DISCOVER AMERICA

From Sea to Shining Sea

ILLUSTRATIONS BY JULIE OLSON

LYRICS BY KATHARINE LEE BATES

SHADOW
MOUNTAIN

For all the men and women who have proudly served
our country. May God shed his grace on thee.
—JO

Oh, beautiful

for spacious skies,

For amber waves of grain,

For purple mountain majesties

Above the fruited plain!

America!

America!

God shed his grace on thee,

And crown thy good

with brotherhood

From sea to shining sea.

1. On the Pier
   Pacific Beach, California
2. Arch Rock
   Valley of Fire State Park, Nevada
3. Freedom Festival Balloon Fest
   Provo, Utah
4. Grand Teton National Park
   Jackson Hole, Wyoming
5. Ski Resort
   Vail, Colorado
6. Corn Fields
   Great Bend, Kansas
7. Gateway Arch
   St. Louis, Missouri
8. Wrigley Field
   Chicago, Illinois
9. Lincoln State Park
   Lincoln City, Indiana
10. Amish Country
    Millersburg, Ohio
11. Independence Hall
    Philadelphia, Pennsylvania
12. The Statue of Liberty
    New York City, New York

To discover MORE of America . . .

Launch Your Balloon

Grab a parent, teacher, or trusted adult and go online
to enhance your experience with this book.

www.DiscoverAmericaBook.com

- Send your own virtual balloon to friends or family members, who can then send it on.

- Discover and track on the website your balloon's progress as it floats across the United States.

- Discover facts for fun or for school reports by clicking on each state.

- Print out coloring pages from the website for each state's flag, flower, and bird.

- Discover what you know about the book and other places in the United States by taking the online quiz.

- Discover on the website a video of the illustrator, Julie Olson, painting and talking about the book.

Illustrations © 2014 Julie Olson

Visit us at ShadowMountain.com

Library of Congress Cataloging-in-Publication Data
Bates, Katharine Lee, 1859–1929, author.
    Discover America : from sea to shining sea / Katharine Lee Bates; illustrated by Julie Olson.
        pages cm
ISBN 978-1-60907-855-3 (hardbound: alk. paper)
1. United States—Juvenile poetry. 2. United States—Pictorial works—Juvenile literature. 3. Patriotic music—United States—Juvenile literature. 4. Picture books for children.
I. Olson, Julie, 1976– illlustrator. II. Title.
PS1077.B4A8 2014
    811'.4—dc23
                                                                                2013039434

Printed in China   1/2014
R.R. Donnelley, Shenzhen, Guangdong, China

10 9 8 7 6 5 4 3 2 1